Whether you are a card-carrying member of the NRA and fully-committed QAnon believer that will help *Make America Great Again* or a Bernie pinky that still believes Hillary is the true President in exile, this book of Trumpisms is something you should carry with you at all times.

These words of back-combed wisdom will either be your bible, codified gems of genius that help you make sense of this brave new world, or they will be infuriating examples of embarrassing ignorance that form the backbone of your argument as to why this enigma should never have become leader of the free world.

Either way, you cannot argue that there is no one like Trump. This is Trump in his own words, how he sees the world and some of the people that inhabit it. We have picked the best of the bunch for you.

Go forth wall-builders. Enjoy.

"You know, it really doesn't matter what the media write ...

... as long as you've got a young, and beautiful, piece of ass."

Interview
Esquire, 1991

TOP TRUMPS

The 'bigly' book of
tremendous Trump quotes

III Clink
Street

London | New York

Published by Clink Street Publishing 2020

Copyright © 2020

First edition.

ISBN: 978-1-913568-94-8
E-Book: 978-1-913568-95-5

"An 'extremely credible source' has called my office and told me that Barack Obama's birth certificate is a fraud."

Twitter
@realDonaldTrump
2012

"I will be so good to women."

CNN
August 2015

"Robert Pattinson should not take back Kristen Stewart. She cheated on him like a dog & will do it again – just watch. He can do much better!"

Twitter
@realDonaldTrump
2012

"I really just see the bigness of it all."

Interview
Associated Press

"I will build a great wall – and nobody builds walls better than me, believe me – and I'll build them very inexpensively. I will build a great, great wall on our southern border, and I will make Mexico pay for that wall. Mark my words."

Presidential Campaign
Announcement Speech

"I'm intelligent. Some people would say I'm very, very, very intelligent."

Fortune
April, 2000

1 1

"When Mexico sends its people, they're not sending the best. They're not sending you, they're sending people that have lots of problems and they're bringing those problems with us. They're bringing drugs. They're bring crime. They're rapists... And some, I assume, are good people."

In a speech announcing his candidacy
June 2015

DONALD ERES UN PENDEJO

FROM ILEGAL MEZCAL

"Our great African-American President hasn't exactly had a positive impact on the thugs who are so happily and openly destroying Baltimore."

Twitter
@realDonaldTrump
2015

"Our not very bright Vice President, Joe Biden, just stated that I wanted to "carpet bomb" the enemy. Sorry Joe, that was Ted Cruz!"

Twitter
@realDonaldTrump
July 2016

"If I were running 'The View', I'd fire Rosie O'Donnell. I mean, I'd look at her right in that fat, ugly face of hers, I'd say 'Rosie, you're fired!'"

ET, 2006

"Bernie's exhausted, he just wants to shut down and go home to bed!"

Twitter
@realDonaldTrump
July 2016

"Something very important, and indeed society changing, may come out of the Ebola epidemic that will be a very good thing: NO SHAKING HANDS!"

Twitter
@realDonaldTrump
2014

"The worst thing a man can do is go bald.

Never let yourself go bald."

From *Never Enough*
Michael D'Antonio

"All of the women on The Apprentice flirted with me - consciously or unconsciously. That's to be expected."

How To Get Rich
2004

"The beauty of me is that I'm very rich."

ABC Interview
2011

"It's freezing and snowing in New York – we need global warming!"

Twitter
@realDonaldTrump
2012

"Arianna Huffington is unattractive both inside and out. I fully understand why her former husband left her for a man - he made a good decision."

Twitter
@realDonaldTrump
2012

"I've said if Ivanka weren't my daughter, perhaps I'd be dating her."

The View
2006

"I have a great relationship with African Americans.

And they like me. I like them."

Anderson Cooper 360
2015

"My fingers are long and beautiful, as, it has been well documented, are various other parts of my body."

Page Six
2011

"You're disgusting."

Trump to the opposing lawyer during a court case when she asked for a medical break to pump breast milk for her three-month-old daughter.

Reported by CNN

"They [ISIS] honour Obama.

In fact, Obama is the founder of ISIS."

Rally in Florida
August 2016

"The point is, you can never be too greedy."

The Art of the Deal
By Donald Trump

"My Twitter has become so powerful that I can actually make my enemies tell the truth."

Twitter
@realDonaldTrump

"Oftentimes when I was sleeping with one of the top women in the world I would say to myself, thinking about me as a boy from Queens, 'Can you believe what I am getting?'"

Think Big
2008

"Look at those hands, are they small hands? And, [Republican rival Marco Rubio] referred to my hands: 'If they're small, something else must be small.' I guarantee you there's no problem. I guarantee."

GOP Debate
March, 2016

"I think the only difference between me and the other candidates is that I'm more honest and my women are more beautiful."

New York Times
1999

"Lyin' Ted Cruz just used a picture of Melania from a shoot in his ad. Be careful, Lyin' Ted, or I will spill the beans on your wife!"

Twitter
@realDonaldTrump
March 2016

"Sorry losers and haters but my IQ is one of the highest – and you all know it! Please don't feel so stupid or insecure; it's not your fault."

Twitter
@realDonaldTrump
May 2013

On exporting
goods to China:

**"Listen you m--
---f------, we're
going to tax you
25 percent!"**

Las Vegas
2011

"I get a standing ovation...

...Other people don't."

Speech, Iowa Summit
2015

"Laziness is a trait in the blacks..."

Alleged quote attributed to Trump published in a book by a former Trump company President.

I have a great relationship with the blacks. I've always had a great relationship with the blacks.

Albany's Talk Radio
1300, April 2011

"Rosie O'Donnell's disgusting both inside and out. You take a look at her, she's a slob. She talks like a truck driver, she doesn't have her facts, she'll say anything that comes to her mind. Her show failed when it was a talk show, the ratings went very, very, very low and very bad, and she got essentially thrown off television. I mean she's basically a disaster."

The Insider, ET

"Hillary Clinton was the worst Secretary of State in the history of the United States. There's never been a Secretary of State so bad as Hillary. The world blew up around us. We lost everything, including all relationships."

NBC News
2015

"If you can't get rich dealing with politicians, there's something wrong with you."

Speech, South Caroline
July 2015

"Free trade is terrible. Free trade can be wonderful if you have smart people. But we have stupid people [in office]."

Announcement Speech
2015

"He's not a war hero. He's a war hero because he was captured. I like people that weren't captured, OK, I hate to tell you."

Speech, Iowa Summit
2015

"I'm the worst thing that's ever happened to ISIS."

Trump to Barbara
Walters in December
2015

On Carly Fiorina

"Look at that face! Would anyone vote for that? Can you imagine that, the face of our next president?"

Rolling Stone
September 2015

I think apologizing's a great thing, but you have to be wrong. I will absolutely apologize, sometime in the hopefully distant future, if I'm ever wrong.

The Tonight Show
September 2015

When these people walk in the room, they don't say, 'Oh, hello! How's the weather? It's so beautiful outside. Isn't it lovely? How are the Yankees doing? Oh they're doing wonderful. Great.' [Asians] say, 'We want deal!'

Rally in Iowa
August 2015

53

On Heidi Klum...

"Sadly, she's no longer a 10."

New York Times
August 2015

"You could see there was blood coming out of her eyes. Blood coming out of her... wherever."

Re Megyn Kelly on CNN interview, August 2015

Megyn Kelly:
"You've called women you don't like 'fat pigs,' 'dogs,' 'slobs,' and 'disgusting animals'..."

Trump: **"Only Rosie O'Donnell."**

GOP Debate
August 2015

"When Mexico sends its people, they're not sending the best...They're rapists and some, I assume, are good people, but I speak to border guards and they're telling us what we're getting."

In a speech announcing his candidacy
June 2015

"You know who's one of the great beauties of the world, according to everybody? And I helped create her. Ivanka. My daughter, Ivanka. She's 6 feet tall, she's got the best body."

Howard Stern Show
August 2003

"It's like in golf. A lot of people – I don't want this to sound trivial – but a lot of people are switching to these really long putters, very unattractive. It's weird. You see these great players with these really long putters, because they can't sink three-footers anymore. And, I hate it. I am a traditionalist. I have so many fabulous friends who happen to be gay, but I am a traditionalist."

Explaining his stance on gay marriage in a *New York Times* profile piece in May 2011

"The line of 'Make America Great Again,' the phrase, that was mine, I came up with it about a year ago, and I kept using it, and everybody's using it, they are all loving it. I don't know I guess I should copyright it, maybe I have copyrighted it."

Trump, claiming that he was the first person to coin the phrase in March 2015. Ronald Reagan used the slogan over 35 years ago during his campaign.

"I will be the greatest jobs president that God ever created."

Trump Tower
Announcing his
candidacy, June 2015

"@cher - I don't wear a "rug" - it's mine. And I promise not to talk about your massive plastic surgeries that didn't work."

Twitter
@realDonaldTrump
2012

"If Hillary Clinton can't satisfy her husband, what makes her think she can satisfy America?"

Twitter - later deleted
2015

"I dealt with Gaddafi. I rented him a piece of land. He paid me more for one night than the land was worth for two years, and then I didn't let him use the land. That's what we should be doing. I don't want to use the word 'screwed,' but I screwed him. That's what we should be doing."

Fox News
2012

"My favorite part [of 'Pulp Fiction'] is when Sam has his gun out in the diner and he tells the guy to tell his girlfriend to shut up. Tell that bitch to be cool. Say: 'Bitch be cool.' I love those lines."

TrumpNation
2005

"I would never buy Ivana any decent jewels or pictures. Why give her negotiable assets?"

Vanity Fair interview
1990

On Foreign Policy

"I'm speaking with myself."

When interviewed by Morning Joe's Mika Brzezinski

"I talk to a lot of people. And at the appropriate time, I'll tell you who the people are. But my primary consultant is myself. And I have a good instinct for this stuff."

On his advisor for
devising Foreign Policy

"The show is 'Trump.' And it is sold-out performances everywhere."

Playboy
1990

"I'm gonna be so presidential that you people will be so bored.

**And people will say...
"Boy he really looks presidential"**

Speech,
Harrisburg, PA

"When was the last time anybody saw us beating, let's say, China in a trade deal? They kill us. I beat China all the time. All the time."

Candidacy
Announcement Speech
2015

"I will build a great wall – and nobody builds walls better than me, believe me –and I'll build them very inexpensively. I will build a great, great wall on our southern border, and I will make Mexico pay for that wall. Mark my words."

Candidacy
Announcement Speech
2015

"Hillary Clinton was the worst Secretary of State in the history of the United States. There's never been a Secretary of State so bad as Hillary. The world blew up around us. We lost everything, including all relationships. There wasn't one good thing that came out of that administration or her being Secretary of State."

NBC Interview
2015

"I saw a report yesterday. There's so much oil, all over the world, they don't know where to dump it. And Saudi Arabia says, 'Oh, there's too much oil.' Do you think they're our friends? They're not our friends."

ABC News Interview
2011

"It's Friday. How many bald eagles did wind turbines kill today? They are an environmental & aesthetic disaster."

Twitter, 2012
@realDonaldTrump

"Amazing how the haters & losers keep tweeting the name "F**kface Von Clownstick" like they are so original & like no one else is doing it..."

F**kface Von Clownstick was a name given to Trump by comedian and Daily Show host Jon Stewart.

"@BetteMidler talks about my hair but I'm not allowed to talk about her ugly face or body --- so I won't. Is this a double standard?"

Twitter, 2012
@realDonaldTrump

"I'm owned by the people! I mean, I'm telling you, I'm no angel, but I'm gonna do right by them!"

Rolling Stone
Steptember 2015

"I have a total grasp of the details – far greater than just about anybody else, that I can tell you."

On ISIS and using
Nuclear Weapons
NBC's TODAY

"I mean, we could say politically correct that look doesn't matter, but the look obviously matters… like you wouldn't have your job if you weren't beautiful."

The Strip View
2014

"I am somebody with a lot of heart."

Washington Examiner

"I think we've done more than perhaps any president in the first 100 days."

Washington Examiner

"I will take care of women. I respect women."

CNN Debate
2015

On September
11th

**"I think I could
have stopped it."**

Hannity
2015

On his first 100 days

"I'd give us an A."

Washington Examiner

"I have black guys counting my money! I hate it. The only kind of people I want counting my money are short guys that wear yarmulkes every day."

Conversation with John O'Donnell recounted in *Trumped*

"I think Reince has been doing an excellent job."

Associated Press

But then...

"I would like to thank Reince Priebus for his service and dedication to his country."

Twitter
@realDonaldTrump

"President Xi [of China], we have a, like, a really great relationship."

Associated Press

"I've passed a lot of legislative bills that people don't even know about."

Washington Post

"Hey, I'm a nationalist and a globalist. I'm both."

Wall Stree Journal

"Jared Kushner did very well yesterday in proving he did not collude with the Russians. Witch Hunt. Next up, 11 year old Barron Trump!"

Twitter
@realDonaldTrump

"Despite the constant negative press covfefe"

Twitter
@realDonaldTrump

"Don't believe the main stream (fake news) media. The White House is running VERY WELL. I inherited a MESS and am in the process of fixing it."

Twitter
@realDonaldTrump

"Can you imagine what the outcry would be if @ SnoopDogg, failing career and all, had aimed and fired the gun at President Obama? Jail time!"

Twitter
@realDonaldTrump

"I would bring back waterboarding and I'd bring back a hell of a lot worse than waterboarding."

Republican Presidential
Debate, ABC News 2016

"I thought it would be easier."

On being President

Reuters

"We have it totally under control. It's one person coming in from China, and we have it under control. It's going to be just fine."

Coronavris Briefing
January 2020

"There was no collusion. Everybody knows there was no collusion."

CNN

"Nobody has better respect for intelligence than Donald Trump."

Press conference at his
Trump National Golf
Club in New Jersey

"I think we've done more than perhaps any president in the first 100 days."

Washington Examiner

"Nobody has better respect for intelligence than Donald Trump."

Press conference at his
Trump National Golf
Club in New Jersey

"Will someone from his [Kim Jung-Un] depleted and food starved regime please inform him that I too have a Nuclear Button, but it is a much bigger & more powerful one than his, and my Button works!"

Twitter

"Why are we having all these people from s**thole countries come here?"

Business Insider

"Lowest rated Oscars in HISTORY. Problem is, we don't have Stars anymore - except your President (just kidding, of course)!"

Twitter

"I'll probably will do it, maybe definitely."

On calling Coranavirus a national emergency

Business Insider

"Anybody that needs a test gets a test. We – they're there. They have the tests. And the tests are beautiful."

On Coronavirus tests - briefing

"Looks like by April, you know, in theory, when it gets a little warmer, it miraculously goes away... But we're doing great in our country... And I think it's going to all work out fine."

On Coranavirus

February 2020
Trump Rally, NH

"If anyone is looking for a good lawyer, I would strongly suggest that you don't retain the services of Michael Cohen!"

Twitter

"No Smocking Gun... No Collusion."

Another covfefe moment

Business Insider

"I beat China all the time. All the time!"

Twitter

"No Smocking Gun... No Collusion."

Another covfefe moment

Business Insider

"Greta must work on her Anger Management problem, then go to a good old fashioned movie with a friend! Chill Greta, Chill!"

Twitter

"I could be the most popular person in Europe. I could be -- I could run for any office if I wanted to, but I don't want to."

Cabinet meeting

"The buck stops with everybody."

The South Lawn

"It's like you'll go 'person, woman, man, camera, TV.'
So they say, 'Could you repeat that?'
So I said 'Yeah.' So it's 'person, woman, man, camera, TV.'"

Explaining his fantastic IQ test results

Fox News interview

"I have no intention of EVER running for president."

TIME Interview
1987

Others in the Series

amazon

www.ingramcontent.com/pod-product-compliance
Lightning Source LLC
Chambersburg PA
CBHW031626040426
42452CB00007B/697